GROWING MY FAITH GARDEN

STARTING WITH THE FRUITS OF THE SPIRIT

Written by Mary Tisdale Green
Scripture look-up by Brock Green
Helping with the fruit of the spirit:
Dominique and Iyania Giles

Order this book online at www.trafford.com
or email orders@trafford.com

Most Trafford titles are also available at major online book retailers.

Printed in the United States of America.

ISBN: 978-1-4669-1169-7 (sc)
ISBN: 978-1-4669-1170-3 (e)

Trafford rev. 10/25/2012

 www.trafford.com

North America & international
toll-free: 1 888 232 4444 (USA & Canada)
phone: 250 383 6864 ◆ fax: 812 355 4082

Hebrews 11:1 says, "Faith is the substance of things hoped for and the evidence of things not seen." Faith is a belief, and it is the size of a mustard seed. Romans 10:17 says, "Faith comes by hearing and hearing by the word of God."

This all started when I was thinking about how a garden grows. My husband is a gardener, and he has some of the most beautiful gardens. I have learned many things about growing a garden from him. I began to think about how the process of growing a physical garden relates to growing a spiritual garden. It is important to me for my children to know how to grow faith and to get started now, rather than waiting until they are older. As we already know, faith comes by hearing and hearing by the word of God. There are people who have been in church all their lives and still do not know how to grow faith.

So this book is important to all. God will supply our every need but will also give us our hearts' desires.

Proverbs 22:6 says, "Train up a child in the way he should go, and when he is older he will not depart." I want faith children, and I want them to know how to grow their faith. They will not have to wish they had this or that, but they can go into the word of God and grow by faith what they need or want.

I am teaching my children this principle. I have learned so much and want to share it with others. Scripture says in Habakkuk 2:2, "Write the vision and make it plain upon tables, that he may run that readeth it." This includes even the children so they will understand.

For years, I heard the word of God, but I did not understand it. I kept praying and asking God to open up my understanding.

.

The late missionary Mae Lois Monroe started a class and called it student night. She often said that if no one else received or learned from that class, Mary Francis did. It was true. I began to mix the word with my everyday life by faith, and God began to open up his wisdom and understanding to me.

I was riding down Congress Avenue one evening in Austin, Texas. I was stopped at the light when God revealed to me that I had once understood in little letters of the alphabet, but I now read in capital letters. I wanted to get out of that car and run around it. But I realized that people now have cell phones and someone would have called 911 and said, "A woman is running around her car at this light on Congress." So I just decided to praise him where I was. Thank you, Lord.

My garden begins first with me deciding what I want to grow: love, joy, peace, meekness, gentleness, goodness, long-suffering, and self-control. My next step is to go to the Bible and get some seeds. The word of God is seed. I look through all scripture for which fruit I want to grow. Finding the right seeds is important.

It is also important for me to know that I can go into the word of God and find seed to grow what I want or need in my life. I have heard testimonies, and I have witnessed in my own life the word of God coming off the pages of the Bible and coming to pass. Growing quality fruit is another important point.

Being around negative people can ruin your garden. Being around complaining people can ruin your garden. So be careful what you put in your garden.

You may say, "But they are my friends!" Maybe you need new friends. We are influenced by others, whether for good or bad. We have to guard our gardens. Have you ever been around people who curse a lot? When you leave them, you may not say the words they say, but you can hear them in your mind and thoughts.

If I am just interested in growing any kind of fruit, I do not have to be concerned about the quality. I am a Christian, and it is important to me that others see Christ in me. By the way, my garden is my heart.

The word of God produces the best fruit. Galatians 5:22 says, "But the fruit of the spirit is love, joy, peace, long-suffering, kindness, goodness, faithfulness, gentleness, and self-control."

The fruit of the spirit is the character of God, and this is the character we, as believers, should have. To grow this character in my life, I go to the word of God to choose these seeds.

But before I can plant my seeds, I need to prepare my garden by plowing up the ground of my garden (my heart). Jeremiah 4:3 says to plow up the hard ground of your heart. Do not waste your good seeds among thorns.

I need to get rid of the weeds and grass in my garden (my heart), so I first ask God to forgive me for all the wrongs I have done. This is turning over the ground of my garden (heart). Forgiving others for the hurt they have caused me helps me to get healing for myself and forgiveness for those I have hurt. The scripture says I must first forgive to get forgiveness (Matthew 6:14 and Mark 11:25). Forgiving others is not a matter of choice; it is a direct command from our Lord that some seem to prefer to ignore or rationalize away. I pull off the old man and get rid of my old ways, and with God's help, I am a new creature, transformed by the renewing of my mind.

I now need to fertilize the ground before I start to plant. I start by working on my relationship by regular Bible studying, meditation, and prayer.

My personal "relationship time" is most important to produce a growing, exciting Christian relationship. Without it, my life will be no different from that of anyone who does not know God. If I do not spend time with God, my relationship with the Lord will stagnate.

It will take practice and patience to establish your relationship time as a life habit rather than just a sporadic event. Think of your relationship time as a personal outing with the Lord each day. The time and the place are vital! I am a night owl, so I read, study, and listen to videos, sometimes all night long.

When you buy a bag of fertilizer, it is already balanced with everything you need. Balance in your life is vital to good growth too. Here are some other important fertilizing parts.

Study of God's Word

The first ingredient is Bible reading. The word of God is food for the soul. Without it, you become empty. Without spiritual nourishment, balance is impossible.

There are higher heights and deeper depths in Christ Jesus. Growth comes from personal encounter with God's word, bringing about revelations. Rather than just a verse or two, you need a healthy portion of God's word for spiritual growth. Just like for me, God will open up your understanding of scripture as you continue to pray and ask him to open up your understanding.

Meditation

Meditation is the second ingredient. Meditating on what you have read keeps what you have studied in your mind. Reading is to hearing what meditation is to listening. Think, ponder, and digest what God is saying to you. Then you apply the scripture to your life. Watch the word of God come off the pages and alive in your life as you practice living in him.

Relationship time is not a ritual but a relationship. You will find that God talks to you as you meditate on his word.

Prayer

Prayer, the third ingredient of relationship time, is talking to God. You'll have many things to talk over with him. Prayer is that fertilizer that conditions the heart to be ready for the seed, which is the word of God. When prayer is worked into the heart along with the seed of the word of God, it will produce a healthy garden and develop a relationship with him.

Your relationship time needs to become a habit as regular as your mealtime. You are not going to miss too many meals. Daily time with God puts muscle on your character. Habits, good or bad, become part of your character as you practice them. I was a cigarette smoker. When Virginia Slims came out, I thought that a cigarette sure did look good, so I bought me a pack and started smoking. Before I knew it, I was no longer in control of smoking; instead, smoking was in control of me. It was now time to stop, and I did. The habit did not start overnight and did not go away overnight. Your relationship time helps you grow to become all that Christ wants you to be.

Praise

The fourth ingredient is praise. You know how good God is and has been to you. Showing your gratitude shows the warmth of your relationship. Praise is a song of thanks in your heart. Without this, your relationship time narrows to a boring rut. Praise reminds me of the person I have chosen to spend time with. Praise is my relationship time appetizer. There is a song that says praise is what I do; I say praise is who I am.

Our spiritual lives grow best when we eat spiritual food, the word of God. *Bon appétit.*

It is time to plant.

One thing I forgot to mention is that for my garden to grow, I have to stay open to hearing his word, reading his word, meditating on his word, and speaking his word so that my garden gets plenty of sun (son).

Sun (Jesus shining in our lives) and water (that living water) will determine how I grow. Will I be stunted because I did not get enough of the sun and water? It will be up to me to make sure I read and study God's word for continued growth.

The Holy Spirit's creative power anoints us with power and growth, just as water and sun anoint plants with life. (1 Corinthians 3:6,) says, I have planted, apollos watered; but God gave the increase. When God fills us with his spirit, we become productive sowers and reapers. Without his anointing, we will be powerless and will not produce spiritually.

Each person's heart is the garden in which the spiritual fruit grows. When the heart condition isn't right, no plant will be able to grow fully. A receptive garden will yield a plentiful harvest, whereas an unreceptive garden will barely yield any before the seed is snatched away by the wrong priorities of life. "Some fell on stoney places, where they has not much earth: and forthwith they sprung up, because they had no deepness of earth: It sprang up quickly, because the soil was shallow" (Matthew 13:5).

The word of God is the seed that can grow into tall plants in a person's heart (garden), depending on the garden's condition (Mark 4:1-20) read for yourself. We need the seed in our heart in order for it to grow into fruit.

All of these are required to reap a great harvest: the son, who is our light; the Holy Spirit, which is our water; our heart, which is the garden; and the word of God that is the seed. "And he shall be like a tree planted by the rivers of water, that brought forth its fruit in its season, whose leaf also doth not wither; and whatsoever he doeth shall prosper" (Psalm 1:3).

"This book of the law shall not depart out of thy mouth, but thou shalt meditate thereon day and night, that thou mayest observe to do according to all that is written therein: for then thou shalt make thy way prosperous, and then thou shalt have good success" (Joshua 1:8).

"But be ye doers of the word, and not hearers only, deluding your own selves. For if anyone is a hearer of the word and not a doer, he is like unto a man beholding his natural face in a mirror: for he beholdeth himself, and goeth away, and straightway forgetteth what manner of man he was. But he that looketh into the perfect law, the law of liberty, and so continueth, being not a hearer that forgetteth but a doer that worketh, this man shall be blessed in his doing" (James 1:22-25).

Jesus said, "I am the true vine, and my father is the husbandman. Every branch in me that beareth not fruit, he taketh it away: and every branch that beareth fruit, he cleanseth it, that it may bear more fruit" (John 15:1-2).

Planting and caring for the seed in our garden guarantees harvest. Meditating on the word of God, the Bible, will promise success. Yet, just reading the Bible does not do it. We must apply his word to our daily living. We must meditate on the word by both hearing and doing. If wrong priorities, unimportant cares of this world, and bad associations are hindering our fruit-bearing, we must get rid of them (prune them) so we can effectively bear the fruit.

These fruits are special because they are supernatural. No one can develop them by his or her self-effort. One fruit is a love that transcends all boundaries, that does not change along with life's circumstances, that endures forever. Since this is a spiritual fruit, it can withstand time, age, and challenges of life. No one will be able to steal it and gobble it all up! And no disease will be able to destroy it as long as you maintain it in good ground.

As believers, we are spirit, soul, and body. We need to live out of our spirit and allow it to lead and direct us. If we allow the spirit to convert our souls, our gardens will grow and grow.

The season is right on the day you hear my voice harden not your heart. We are not too young to give our hearts to God.

Let's get these rows of fruit planted. We have nine rows to plant. Let's hear the word of God.

These are the nine rows I am planting in my garden.

Our first row is love. John 3:16 says, "For God so loved the world that he gave his one and only son, that whoever believes in him shall not perish but have eternal life."

God is love. Love is an emotion of strong affection and personal attachment. It is also a virtue representing all of human kindness, compassion, unselfish loyalty, and benevolent concern for others.

At one point in my life, I was so full of hurt and anger. I understood what it meant to say that there is a thin line between love and hate. God put a baby in my life to teach me how to grow real love, not emotional love. This is why it is so important to have the Holy Ghost. Our love only goes so far. God's love, *agape* love, takes over and goes beyond what we would ever think. Now I am like this red, juicy apple. If you take a bite out of me, you will get juiciness.

The next row is peace. Let the peace of God rest, rule, and abide in your heart.

Peace is a state of harmony. Peace also suggests the existence of a healthy or newly healed interpersonal relationship with God.

I love this revelation. As I meditated on it, I could see myself growing as I allowed the word of God to rest, rule, and abide in me. I planted peace, and it spread out all over my life.

The next row of fruit is joy. Nehemiah 8:10 says, "The joy of the Lord is my strength." Joy is eternal. Joy is the emotion evoked by wellbeing or success; it is a state of happiness, a source or cause of delight. To grow this fruit, I started delighting myself in the Lord. We sing the song "Little Sally Walker": "Put your whole self in, and that is what it is all about."

The next fruit is long-suffering. Long-suffering is putting up with difficulties, being patient, endurance during trials or trouble. Anyone can start to go through something, but can you finish? I thank God for that go-through spirit. It takes patience to wait on God.

Our next fruit is gentleness. Gentleness is a way of life, showing our love in how we interact with people. People are souls and very important to God, and this is the way we should treat others.

Next we have goodness. Goodness is a state of being good, kind, honest, generous, and helpful. I believe in treating others as I want to be treated. I am good to others on purpose.

Next we have faith. Faith is confidence or trust in someone or a belief in God. I am out of the box and on the bus watching God by faith bring things to pass in my life. I am out of the religious box and living by God's word.

Our next fruit is temperance. Temperance is self-restraint in action, self-control. Years ago, God taught me temperance through sewing. I learned that you have to cut out the pattern, lay it on material, pin it down, cut it out, sew pieces together, and make adjustments. After learning to sew, I have temperance.

Next we have meekness. Meekness is compatible with high spirit, courage, and great strength. That is exactly what the word of God has done for me. The word has grown courage and strength in me. Thank you, Lord.

I am watching my fruit as it grows in my garden, my husband's garden, and my children and grandchildren's gardens.

Luke 22:32 says, "But I have prayed for you, Simon, that your faith may not fail." When you are strengthened, strengthen your brother, sister, people you meet, children, and all.

Romans 13:14 says, "Rather, clothe yourselves with the Lord Jesus Christ." It is time we put on the Lord Jesus and wear him so that as we plant seeds in our garden (our hearts), not only will we expect a harvest, but we will receive a harvest.

Growing our fruit of the sprit garden is just the beginning of our work. We will not go to bed a blunder and wake up a wonder, but we need to get started. What about now? Let's start with love and allow prayer mixed with the word of God to penetrate our hearts and then meditate on each of these fruits until it is bursting out in us. We will be looking in the mirror of God's word and seeing ourselves by faith until we can see ourselves as God sees us.

May this book inspire you to eat from these fruits until you are dripping in fruit juices.

I pray that you become so hungry to be like Jesus that nothing less will satisfy.

May God's anointing bless you as you read this book.

I want to thank my husband, Brock, and my grandchildren, Dominique and Iyania, who inspire me to write as I live. Philippians 1:21 says, "For to me, to live is Christ and to die is gain." To live is Christ. Thank you, family.

A special thanks to Flo Rice Tisdale and missionary Lisa Patterson, elect lady at Morning Glory Church of God in Christ, for proofreading for me. Thanks, ladies.